"*Interrogation Records* by Jeddie Sophronius [illegible] personal and political at a scale that lets us observe [illegible] the reader as they traverse that bridge. As a poet and researcher, I have wanted more US-based presses to publish documentary works that address underexpressed and understudied historical events that have taken place outside the United States. I have wanted us to expand our conversation about genocide, politicide, ethno-racial beliefs and prejudice, and the charge against communism out in open fora, especially through poetry. And I see in Jeddie's book precisely such an occasion for us to have an expanded conversation. *Interrogation Records* responds to the systematic killings in Indonesia that took place between 1965 and 1966. Under Suharto's regime, the Indonesian army was responsible for civil unrest and the slaughter of civilians who were alleged members of the Communist Party—civilians who were sympathetic to the feminist, anti-imperialist, pro-labor Gerwani women's organization, trade unionists, and ethnic and religious minorities, including Javanese Abangan Muslims, ethnic Chinese, and atheists. Some estimates suggest that 3 million were killed that year.

Jeddie's book is a keen, sparse, documentary approach to archival records. Yet it is not bloodless or without passion. The most significant documentary poetry tethers us to the historic event with the poetic line as if it were our very sinews. It implicates us at the arteries, it calls us into an enfleshed attachment. It enlivens the dead texts of archives, reanimates them so that we recall and revere the human lives that they document. It intentionally shapes verse and prose so that that our own relationship with the historical event is not dominated by habitual and superficial empathy, but is built slowly through the greater facilities that reading can engender: curiosity, critical judgment, generous discernment born of difficulty, and a luminous attention to bureaucratic language which structures yet obscures so much of our social existence. I see in Jeddie's book a significant aspiration towards these important achievements, so often evident in the work of Muriel Rukeyser and Charles Reznikoff. Yet his book is also a preserving of an activist vernacular that we admire in the Black Arts movement, embodied in the perspicuous countenance of the speakers in the poetry of Sonia Sanchez, Etheridge Knight, and June Jordan. At its most exciting moments, Jeddie's *Interrogation Records* is inflected by the work of poets of Southeast Asian descent in US-anglophone contexts like Diana Khoi Nguyen and Mai Der Vang. He is writing into the growing library of Asian writers in the United States whose literary work attends to genocide, war, and political incarceration, advancing both a journalistic and a research-oriented poetics within this diasporic formation.

In his poem "The Sinner's Mantra" Jeddie quotes the adage from Karl Marx's "Critique of the Gotha Program": "From each according to their ability, to each according to their need." And if I may, I would say: Jeddie's great and significant ability, in his book, matches our great and significant need to learn more about the Indonesian killings of 65–66. So, I receive his book as a gift and a redress of silence. And every time we learn history through poetry that intentionally unsilences the archives, we are unwriting a master-narrative, we are writing and reading as a prevention of erasure, we are writing and reading as a cure for amnesia."

—Divya Victor, winner of the
2022 PEN America Open Book Award

"*Interrogation Records* is a stunning work by a keen poetic intellect. Writing at the intersection of history and remembrance, Sophronius contends with the multigenerational aftermath of state violence and the powerful forces of historical erasure. The ongoing inheritance Sophronius excavates in these lyrics is part-memory, part-burden, part-presence, part-silence. Each poem feels hard-won from the mysterious cultural machinery we call "archive," lifted into astonishing, often heartbreaking, utterance. In its possession of the visual field of the page, in its formal rigor, and in its virtuosic expression, Interrogation Records invites us on a remarkable journey."

—Kiki Petrosino, author,
White Blood: A Lyric of Virginia

"*Interrogation Records* lays bare a powerful affective archive of the 1965 mass killings in Indonesia and their aftermath. The poetry collection does not seek to depict the atrocity as an isolated historical event; Jeddie Sophronius instead takes on the more compelling, indeed the more pressing task of trying to understand and express how society remembers and forgets crimes of the state generations after that violence took place. How to make history carry collective meaning, how to make the past felt, how to make documents and archives and testimony hold affective power—these are the questions *Interrogation Records* explores, and indeed the political concerns that most urgently require poetic language. Sophronius constructs a series of dialogues across the multi-layered discourse about 1965, offering insightful critiques of public perception, state ideologies, and propaganda while engaging numerous voices--scholarly, testimonial, ghostly, intimate. From reflections on identity and belonging to biting satire of euphemisms employed by the state to obscure fear, pain, and the striking elimination of human life, *Interrogation Records* is a search for the fragmented traces of memory that scatter present-day Indonesia."

—Lara Norgaard, translator

INTERROGATION RECORDS

INTERROGATION RECORDS

JEDDIE SOPHRONIUS

Published by Gaudy Boy LLC,
an imprint of Singapore Unbound
www.singaporeunbound.org/gaudyboy
New York

For more information on ordering books, contact jkoh@singaporeunbound.org.

ISBN 978-1-958652-07-7
Library of Congress Control Number: 2024933350

Cover design by Flora Chan
Interior design by Jennifer Houle

for my people

Contents

A Signpost

Take nothing from the mountain
   Leave nothing in the mountain

Take nothing from the river
   Leave nothing in the river

I

Indonesia, my homeland
Land where I shed my blood
Over there, I stand
To be my mother's guide

—Indonesia Raya, first verse

Origin of a Disaster

At each building, an army captain read names from a list, advising them of their guilt "in the name of the law".... The neighborhood peasants had been ordered by their headman to dig a large pit the day before. The prisoners, lined up at the edge of the pit, were shot down in a matter of minutes. Some may have been buried alive.

—STANLEY KARNOW, "FIRST REPORT ON HORROR IN INDONESIA",

THE WASHINGTON POST, APR. 17, 1966

Once in a lifetime, a massacre.
Every three massacres or so,
a migration of ghosts. The dead

climb from closed pits or writhe from piles
of limbs. Their children, the ones they
left years ago, wake up sweating

as though they were soaked in rain. Wraiths
gather from the earth and pass through
rice fields, weeping figs, and rumah-

rumah adat. Doors lock, curtains
close. A mother sways her newborn
to sleep, promises the wind will

pass. Once God forgets a country,
rivers disappear, rainforests
burn, a village girl heaves her

daily water from the well, finds
only redness. Each disaster
remains as a reminder to

sujud, beg God to come back. Fast
and repent if you must, repent
now. The sin is already done,

the sin of your fathers, forefathers.
Come here now, sit down, and listen:
the ghosts are here to testify.

Death List

As many as 5,000 names were furnished over a period of months to the army there, and the Americans later checked off the names of those who had been killed or captured, according to the former U.S. officials ... "No one cared, so long as they were communists, that they were being butchered," said Howard Federspiel, who in 1965 was the Indonesia expert at the State Department's bureau of intelligence and research. "No one was getting very worked up about it."

—KATHY KADANE,
"U.S. OFFICIALS' LISTS AIDED INDONESIAN BLOODBATH IN '60S",
THE WASHINGTON POST, MAY 21, 1990

Lives perished, yet
nothing happened.

Earth's rotation
did not stop. It

happened elsewhere,
somewhere distant:

not here. It was
contained, as in

the earthquake was
contained: struck a

place much farther
than the distance

the average man
would care. The dead

3

was not our dead.
The dead were at

     fault. The dead were
our enemies.

     The dead chose wrong.
They weren't alive

     to begin with. Nothing
happened. No one cared.

Killing System

For the most part, the killings were carried out in a systematic and ordered manner: accounts of frenzied or anarchical massacres were rare. Victims' throats were usually cut with knives, sickles or machetes; less commonly, and apparently only when civilians were reluctant to cooperate, the condemned persons were shot by the military.

—GREG FEALY AND KATHARINE MCGREGOR,
THE CONTOURS OF MASS VIOLENCE IN INDONESIA, 1965–1968

One day, lives, waiting
    to be disposed, then
the next, no one was

left. They were killing
    and disposing way
faster than the new

bodies were coming.
    Efficient. Ripe heads,
waiting to be sliced,

like watermelons,
    helpless, round, asking
for the knives to kiss

them. Ordered manner.
    Those were the orders:
to kiss or be kissed.

If they hadn't done
    it, someone else would.
If they hadn't swung

their machetes, something
     else would've killed them.
Very clean. It was

     all systematic.

Numbers, Statistics, Etc.

Mr. Permadi, three million were killed. Most of them on my orders.

—SARWO EDHIE WIBOWO,
COMMANDER OF THE ELITE RPKAD IN 1965, SHORTLY BEFORE HIS DEATH

One million, three million—none
of it mattered. The numbers were just

that: statistics, a simple
addition, marginalia. Lives

disappeared without a trace,
a vanishing of some sort. The earth

couldn't contain the silence,
bodies shattering to dust. Children

stayed quiet as the echoes
roaming the night grew louder. What was

a hum, now a storm. Of course,
the dead screamed—lumps of bodies, covered

in the nothingness of earth.
They all perished, most of them on our orders.

Testimony / Propaganda

The Embassy has received a number of reports concerning arrests of prominent PKI leaders although the evidence is often suspect. There is a widespread falsification of documents such as alleged confessions, some of which can be easily detected and some not.

—CABLE FROM U.S. DEPARTMENT OF STATE
TO U.S. EMBASSY JAKARTA, DEC. 17, 1965

i.
They were communists,
     guilty in their own
   being. Their existence
      a threat to our own,
    like cancer or sin.

ii.
Like cancer or sin,
     they were godless. They
   slept with each other's
      wives, killed anyone
    who opposed their dark
       ideology.

iii.
Ideology—
     ours is the belief
   in the Almighty God,
      it's what makes us strong,
    it's what makes us one.
       As for them, who could
    even imagine?

iv.

Who could imagine
      what they would've done
   to our country, if
         we hadn't dealt with
    the sinners among
          us, those atheists?
       Who could say? They were
       communists.

Interrogation Room

Communists are cruel. Communists don't believe in God.

—COMMON ANTI-COMMUNIST NARRATIVE

There was a table:

the questioned on one side,
                    and the questioner

                on the other. It was

midday, but the subject
        didn't know that.

    His breath

            fell heavy against
                    the black bag

        over his face.

                The man took
                    his baton, laid it

        on the table. The subject

heard the clunk,
        his shoulders

                jumped. Then, the man

laid a cattle prod—
     an electric rod—

the handle rolling

from side to side,
     the questioner

          half-bored, half-testing

its weight. Soon, another man
     in boots brought

          an ekor pari, newly

crafted for the session.
     The first man rose

from his seat, smiled

          to the second man,
               and took the whip

by its white handle.

          He tried a few
     strokes against

               the marble floors

while the other man
          stood and watched.

The subject heard

the thrashing,
   knew what was

      bound to happen.

  Anticipating,
    he raised

      his shoulders

   up to his ears,
like a child

    waiting

     for the belt.
      Cheeks, ears,

        stomach, thighs,

  and other parts
    that he never

    showed to anyone—

     after it was done,
  even his mother

wouldn't recognize him.

Research Process

One book cites a library containing
a collection of oral interviews
with old survivors of the massacre.
Upon looking up that the library

is in my home city, I drive to that
unfamiliar district—passing tight roads
and corners that only fit one car. I
arrive at what looks like a bungalow.

I wave to the person inside. He lets
me in but says he's left the archive's key
back home. I'm the first to visit since
he took his position, some time ago.

*Oh, we don't have a cassette player, bring
your own.* Where can I possibly find one?

II

Indonesia, my nationality
My nation and homeland
Let us exclaim
Indonesia unites!

—INDONESIA RAYA, SECOND VERSE

1965, Indonesia

All the millions of people associated with the PKI, even illiterate peasants in remote villages, were presented as murderers collectively responsible for the movement. Every person detained by the military was accused of being "directly or indirectly involved in the September 30th Movement."

—JOHN ROOSA, PRETEXT FOR MASS MURDER

[The army] was burning down the house to kill a rat.

—SUKARNO, FOUNDING FATHER
AND 1ST PRESIDENT OF INDONESIA, OCT. 27, 1965

We know seven generals were killed,
thus, blood must be shed, a knife for a knife.
A million souls perished in the aftermath,
a massacre—we speak of it no more.

Thus, rivers of blood, knives against knives.
Farmers, fishermen—all alleged communists—
were massacred. We speak of them no more.
Our people killed and mourned in silence.

All alleged communists, young and old,
ceased to exist, like smoke from fireworks.
Our people celebrated in silence.
But why? It never happened.

If you were a communist, you ceased to exist.
Your family couldn't ask what happened.
Why ask? Nothing ever happened.
If you were lucky, you were imprisoned.

17

Your family didn't know what happened,
the soldiers said you never existed.
If you were lucky, you were imprisoned,
your name erased from your mother's tongue.

No one killed anybody, no soldiers existed.
The land could hide so many bodies,
could erase many names from many tongues.
Why bother wondering what happened?

Our country is full of bodies
of those dead not from war but from peace.
Why bother wondering what happened?
Why kill our own?

Our people were slaughtered in a time of peace.
Like helpless chickens, many accepted their fate.
We never ask why we killed our own
acquaintances, colleagues, neighbors.

Like helpless chickens, we didn't know the fate
of a million souls who perished in the aftermath,
killed by their own colleagues and neighbors.
We only know seven generals were killed.

The Sinner's Mantra

The overwhelmingly majority of the victims of the 1965–66 killings were poor, rural people who had aligned themselves with the PKI simply because it was the only political organization which seemed at all interested in representing them, both at a grass-roots, local level, and in the arena of the high politics of Jakarta.

—NATHANIEL MEHR, 'CONSTRUCTIVE BLOODBATH' IN INDONESIA

From each according to their ability,
    to each according to their need.
Ask why the poor have no food.
    Have faith in the masses.
Take your hammers; take your sickles.
    Workers of the world, unite!
Take your hammers; take your sickles.
    Have faith in the masses.
Ask why the poor have no food.
    To each according to their need,
from each according to their ability.

Genjer-Genjer

Genjer-genjer nong kedokan pating keleler
Genjer-genjer nong kedokan pating keleler
Emake thulik teka-teka mbubuti genjer
Emake thulik teka-teka mbubuti genjer
Ulih sak tenong mungkur sedhot sing tulih-tulih
Genjer-genjer saiki wis digawa mulih

—"Genjer-Genjer," first verse

Gather them
   from the muddy streams
      the murky ponds
         and mossy lakes

   Gather genjer-genjer
      Place them
         in your bamboo basket
Bring them home

      Wash them clean
         Tie them with rubber bands
and lay them in rows
   at the market!

      Genjer-genjer
gifts from the land
   What the land gives
      take it

Boil the genjer-genjer
Drain the water
Eat them with rice
and sambal!

Mass Murder

The truth of the matter is that the precise death toll does not alter the nature of the crime: mass murder is mass murder.

—DOUGLAS KAMMEN AND KATHERINE MCGREGOR,
THE CONTOURS OF MASS VIOLENCE IN INDONESIA, 1965–1968

The truth: each massacre remains
nothing but a reminder of our failure
as the human race. The truth: we stood by:
didn't do anything, didn't do shit; stood by

and praised the murderers for their crimes
which they did well, incredibly well; stood by,
as shit evolved into a bigger shit; until
the shit hit our clothes, tuxes, leather shoes;

until the shit turned to blood, stained streets,
cars, houses, court houses, government
buildings. The truth: we didn't know,
we didn't care.

Holy Duty

When those involved in Nahdlatul Ulama's killing squads are asked why they executed communists, the most frequent reply is that their motivation was religious.

—GREG FEALY, *INSIDE INDONESIA*, JAN. 24, 2010

Events in Indonesia might be a little easier to understand if the communists were killed just for their political beliefs and unscrupulous practices. However, their slaughter was largely a religious issue, a power struggle between communist atheism and fanatical Muslims, Hindus and Christians.

—TED YATES, *INDONESIA: THE TROUBLED VICTORY*, 1967

Although [the army] devote[s] considerable time and resources to transform ex-PKI into decent, God-fearing Indonesian citizens, their underlying attitude is "Once a communist, always a communist". They will never accept the fact—and it is a fact—that a large proportion of the members of the PKI and the associated mass organizations were devout Muslims or Christians or adherents to other religious faiths.

—CARMEL BUDIARDJO, *SURVIVING INDONESIA'S GULAG*

What else could it be?   It was propaganda

Killing was a duty   Was sparing lives impossible?
   Killing was the duty   Was mercy impossible?

      They obeyed orders   They didn't have to do it
         They obeyed God   They didn't have to

         We hail them as saviors   We call them killers

      They eliminated enemies,   They killed the innocent:
      enemies of God   people on the wrong

   The opposite of sin is good   side of the narrative
   deed worthy of a reward   civilians mistaken as villains

What else could it be?   It was propaganda

To Kill a Chicken

CN: 184A

DATE: DECEMBER 6, 1965
1120

CONFIDENTIAL 06 DEC 65

ACTION: POL

INFO: CHRON
AMB
DCM
RF
ECON
POL
eg.

Grip its legs
upside down.
Stuff its beak with a rag
        from your neighbor's clothesline.
Tie its wings, strip
each side of its feathers,

Take a kitchen knife or whatever's sharp
and pluck its eyes out. Hold
                    its warm neck
with your fingers.

Run your blade along the lines
that keep the head intact, then down
            the back,
like slicing a watermelon—

        make sure to do this last,
so the chicken is no longer
a chicken
        when you kill it.

1. "CONSCIOUS" PKI MEMBERS ARE
CLASSIFIED AS LOWEST ORDER OF INFIDEL,
THE SHEDDING OF WHOSE BLOOD
IS COMPARABLE TO KILLING CHICKEN.

GP-3
KEAVNER
BT
CFN 338

Research Process

I visit again the very next week,
even though I've yet to find a player.
I peruse the small library: Lenin's

collected essays, books on Japanese
and Dutch occupation, some Javanese
poems, and the lifework of the writer

Pramoedya—alleged communist,
imprisoned on Buru island. I find
a shelf full of his published novels, some

copies of earlier drafts, and letters.
I find six titles I wish to borrow
and ask the librarian if I could.

No, he says and instead promises to
photocopy them for me by next week.

Annotations

Tonight, I can't carry my country's sins.
I've been distant, silent, like any good
researcher. My point of departure. Watch

me bring the "I" into the collective,
the "we" breaking formation from the crowd
until it means "you" and "me." My story

bleeds into the pages of history,
and the story repeats—an hourglass
that I wish will end differently someday.

Now, I will say my piece so that it grows
as one world ends. Sometimes, I think that's all
I've left: a ghost—my memory—living

within these white and red pages. What is
a massacre to the end of the world?

Annotations

I'm returning to
   the origin
      of my grief:

the reason why I
   write: my heartache.
      Because our

relationship has
   ended before
      it began.

Everyone leaves in
   the end, I know
      this, but don't

understand why. When
   I decided
      I wanted

to be with you, I
   knew I declared
      our ending.

Because the apple
   was rotten long
      before the

first bite, therefore our
    love was to be
        our downfall.

Before we confessed,
    before we kissed,
        before we

mapped our nakedness.
    What was it that
        I tried to

say? That we were not
    ready? No, it
        was the world.

The screams, the curses,
    the disowning,
        the cries—I

could hear them before
    I had met you.
        Because there

was no word for our
    existence, we
        molded *us*

out of glass and tears.
    We embraced clothe-
        less: the night

our coat, the walls our
         witness. Because
                  someday, when

we depart, only
         one of us would
                  forget this.

Temple Gate

the   lie
lives   flows
we've cast   in all our
clean   blood
our memory   of sinners

we hide behind   our old amnesia
our soft smiles & nods   a grief we can't utter
we accept the bloodletting   we accept the bloodletting
the heavens allowed it   no room for regret now

soldiers of god   o holy warriors
stay brave   keep watch
the dead remain   wandering souls
await us like vultures   await us to fall open
we don't wish to surrender   our bodies free for taking

we bring offerings to the dead   we try to ease their haunting
on roads where we severed   the living under moonlight
blood & bodies & souls   each night every night

out of our duty
holy duty
for the country

what we did was
a pure &
obligatory deed

between those who died
we took care of the bodies
bathed the dead in the stream
but why does sleep elude us still

we formed madewa pitra
a contract of consequences
carried out our karmic duty &
to this day we fulfill the bargain

if we transgressed forgive us
but don't ask us to regret
don't mention the past
a child sees as
red pouring into a cup
what happened, happened

if we have sinned o forgive us
if we lose hope forgive us
we can't undo anything
like the moment
a dagger kisses a neck
what happened, happened

the heaven gates await us but
our sins shut us from the heavens
please forgive us, forgive us body
& soul

every year we go on as though
this terrible past still haunts us
please forgive us, forgive us body
& soul

Daily Portion

In our area the military would capture the Communist and deliver them to a particular location—usually a secluded place beside a river. The Banser commander would then be told to assemble [his unit] there to do the killings.

—A FORMER BANSER MEMBER

They [the military] said they would release me on one condition: that I dispose the body of those they killed. I had to throw them in the river at night, at least two a night, but on Saturday it was 20 to 25. I did that every year for two years.

—MARTONO, DISPOSED OF BODIES

Offer the river
    a body

Then another
    and another

Offer the river
    your sins

your shame
    your secret

again   and again
    Offer everything

Confess everything
    Let the river

run red   Let the river
   plead and beg

to the ocean
   for emptiness

Reports on the Land

We receive reports of ~~PKI~~ chickens
being slaughtered in many areas.

A missionary, who returned, said
she had seen 25 ~~bodies~~ chickens in the river;

another missionary said he had seen
29 chickens in the same river.

The largest slaughter was,
reportedly, 15,000 ~~communists~~ chickens.

According to numerous sources,
killing of chickens continues in villages.

Wounded chickens released from Surabaya
had refused to return to their homes.

Some railway stations had closed
because workers were afraid

of coming to work since
many chickens were murdered.

Both in the provinces and in Djakarta,
repression of the chickens continues,
with the main problem being that of what
to feed and where to house the chickens.

Many provinces appear to successfully
meet this problem by executing
their chickens or by killing them
before they were captured.

East Java. General pattern
unclear. On one hand, in Kediri,
where chickens have been decimated,
military reportedly seeking
to stop the killings.

On other, in Pasuruan,
where chickens have not been
completely cleaned up, military
still reportedly turning its back
and allowing the slaughter to continue.

The different islands deal
with the chickens in various ways.
In some camps, they are starved to death
or released periodically to be killed
by the local citizens.

Bali has become more beautiful
without chickens. It was the duty
of the Balinese to clean their own
island from chickens. It was a holy
duty, and we did it.

So we dragged the chickens down
this hill. If they didn't want
to be dragged, we threw them.

*

If we hadn't drunk chicken blood,
we would've gone crazy by now.
Many went crazy. . . . Some killed
so many chickens they went crazy.
One man climbed a palm tree
each morning to do the call to prayer.
He killed too many ~~men~~ chickens.
There was only one way to avoid it:
drink the chicken's blood, or go crazy.
It was both salty and sweet, chicken blood.

*

He didn't want to kill his own ~~sister~~ chicken,
so he sent her to me. Yes, he sent her to me.

Every time the truck came,

they took another thirty ~~communists~~
~~prisoners~~
~~people~~
chickens.

I didn't help! I didn't take

a machete and slaughter chickens.

I was told they were bad chickens.

What's more, they never prayed!

In 1965, chickens rushed to the mosques . . .

because they were

afraid of being slaughtered.

Once, I brought a ~~communist's head~~ chicken's head
to a Chinese coffee shop. The Chinese screamed.

You brought a chicken's head?

Yes.

To frighten the Chinese?

Yes. So they'd be scared.

Just to scare them?

Just to scare them.

There are many ghosts here,
because many chickens were killed here.
They died unnatural deaths.

Here was the paramilitary office,
where I always killed chickens.

In the end, I'm disturbed in my sleep.
Maybe because when I strangled
chickens with wire, I watched them die.

The Land's Testimony

After it was all over, who would buy fish?

—INONG, DEATH SQUAD LEADER

You who razed my forests with trucks,
who dug holes in my plains,
who shot chickens for fun,

who made sure children saw the trail
of feathers, who hungered like
hurricane, hungered like lava,

you who took your own countrymen,
who said you were saving them, from
what? the angry mob? the people

sharpening ceremonial
daggers as though preparing for
a sacrifice? you who lied, who

dragged the terrified to prisons
until you could house no more, you
who loaded dozens on your trucks

in darkness, who carried them to
the river's teeth, where the same mob
was waiting, you who were setting

the altar all along, you know
what you committed: you offered
body after body after body after

Research Process

This time, I bring a player. I enter
the archive and find it empty, save for

a single drawer filled with stacks and rows,
hundreds of transparent-cased cassettes, lined,

labeled with a name, arranged by city.
Jogja, Surabaya, Medan . . . I start

with mine. I find one from a survivor
who shares my lost family name, "Chandra"—

the same name father made sure wouldn't get
passed onto his children. When I was born,

he named me without Chandra. My middle
name became my last. I was supposed to

start a new lineage, one where my name
doesn't seem Chinese. Thus, Sophronius.

Annotations

If only you could see yourself through my eyes. And what then, would I see? What scars would your eyes uncut? What fractures would you mend with your touch? What cloudy thoughts would disappear in your embrace? What past would remain buried under my skin? In the end, you too have left this shell I call body, found another to call your own. We made the right choice. Together, we had to fight the world. Alone, I only have to fight our past happiness. Here I am, years later, waiting for the echo of you.

> Slowly
> I am
> loving myself.

IV

Indonesia the Great, be free! Be free!
My land, my country which I love!

—INDONESIA RAYA, REFRAIN

What's your relationship to your subject matter?

The country I call my home
has never been mine. The people

I've shared my meals with
don't want me here. I stay alive

by remaining concealed, my head
forever bowed, my lips still.

I don't make eye contact
with those who could kill me.

All I've ever asked was to love
and be loved in return.

Now, I walk with the weight
of history: terrified of something

that no one I know cares about.

Song of the Chicken

the rulers

that exist

remain

unmoved as they

witness the

chickens

today,

bodies

neglected by

rice.

up in heaven,

ignorant gods

can't explain

why the

lost

hear the

fowls

singing,

we survive

in

the city—

maybe we can mold

a messiah

and start calming

the suffering

gods

and

hungry chickens.

in a prophecy:

we exist

in our cold

cages, forever

in need of

a prophet

to wake

the flood

POL 2-1

Problem	Recommendation
The Communist Party	[Kill ~~or capture~~ all three million members]
The army lacks resources to bridge the archipelago	[Employ propaganda. Turn the people against their neighbors]
Civilians are inexperienced at killing	[Give adequate training to function as death squads]
Civilians lack food	[Allow plundering]
Civilians lack motivation to kill	[Ultimatum: kill or be killed]
Inadequate food for prisoners	[Resolved]
Inadequate space to house prisoners	[Resolved]
Inadequate food	[Resolved]
Inadequate space	[ ]
Inadequate space	[ ]
Inadequate	[ ]

Red All Over

Control: 762A

Recd: December 22, 1965
0700

ACTION:
TOP

INFO:
GENON
AME
MIN
R.F
! CON
CAO
ATTACHE
POL

It is only logical:
those who fled
Red countries bear the mark
of Red itself,

how a chicken remains
a chicken, even
    if you've stripped it
of its feathers.

Our islands were rotten
with Red all over.
Therefore, men
fashioned spears

out of bamboo,
torches out of towels.
They flooded the river
Red.

3. Reports on Bali.
Japanese Consul, who returned from Bali
December 16, said burning of Chinese
stores and shooting at night continues.

Nrimo

I tried to make them accept that they were going to die.

—ADI ZULKADR, EXECUTIONER

To accept everything
coming their way. To understand
an earthquake is the snore of a sleeping god,

and a tsunami is Goddess Ratu Kidul
looking for a new lover. To not mourn
dead children. If a beheaded body

knocks at night, send it
back to the grave, to sleep. Do not
question God's will. Let the dead stay

confused with their missing toes and ankles,
fingers and wrists. Let them count with whatever
they have left. If they can only count

with the lump of a hand, leave it at one
and nothing more. If their children
were murdered, do not blame God

or the killers, the bayonets and sharp wires,
the stray bullets. Say thank you.
Thank you for saving our country.

Public Knowledge

In retrospect, it is easy now to say that our initial interpretation of the "September 30 Movement"—the so-called PKI coup attempt of October 1, 1965—was correct. We knew from the start that it was not a coup in the classic sense.

—RICHARD CABOT HOWLAND, "THE LESSONS OF THE SEPTEMBER 30 AFFAIR",

CENTRAL INTELLIGENCE AGENCY, *STUDIES IN INTELLIGENCE*, 1970

First, I want to deny the idea that "I probably have a lot of blood on my hands; but that's not all bad" ... It is true I passed names of the PKI leaders and senior cadre system to the non-communist forces during the six months of chaos between the so-called coup and the ultimate downfall of Sukarno ... [T]he names I gave were based entirely—I repeat entirely—on the Indonesian communist press and were available to everyone ... The non-communists probably knew much of this information themselves. I don't know.

— ROBERT J. MARTENS, "ACCOUNT OF INDONESIA KILLINGS HIGHLY FLAWED",

THE BUFFALO NEWS, JUN. 12, 1990

Lies on top of deception,
        knowledge hidden beneath knowing—

a foresight, a dark narrative. From the mold
        of one story, another tale awaits.

In all of them, the people in power
        construct their kingdom

on the foundation that everyone else
        complies, that feet remain

in mud and minds in amnesia. A caring
    heart does not sustain

this kingdom, a hungry stomach
    does. Cries, screams, and calls

for justice do not fuel
    the kingdom. Silence does.

Islands of Souls

I.   Kemarin: Bali

Some knew they were going to be killed anyway,
so they approached their killers first and begged for time.

> *Let me sit on the temple stairs, feel the cold stone*
> *against my palms one last time. Let me say goodbye*
> *to my children, tell them to be good. Tomorrow,*
> *I'll offer my body on the village altar.*

Sometimes you would hear screams of pain—or yells to burn,
to kill. The main road was full of curious crowds.
Some let children ride their backs, so they could witness
brown skin folding like mimosa set aflame.

> *This place was truly a heaven on earth. Butchers*
> *embraced their chickens with open arms, promised a*
> *gravestone, then told them to be good in the next life.*

II.   Kini: Sumatra

Here, if you kneel by the riverbank and wait long
enough, you hear murmurs from the stream, echoes.

> *This is the spot. There were boards here. There was a pier.*
> *After the head was cut off, the body was kicked into the river.*
> *Kicked that way. The body would float, so would the head.*
> *Head, body, another head. All bobbed up and down.*

The locals call it Sungai Ular (Snake River).
A silent witness, that's what she is, this river.

> *The past is past.*   *Astaghfirullah.*
> *We've accepted it.*   *Astaghfirullah.*
> *We don't want to remember.*   *Astaghfirullah.*

III.   Esok: Java

Once a year, children will gather in their schoolyard
and watch a film. A number among them will boast
how their grandfathers killed hundreds of red chickens.

> *Be wary of the rise of new communism*
> *that has become more difficult to recognize.*
> *Always be vigilant and deal with the symptoms*

Some will squint during the torture scene: the chickens
taking turns at the bruised man, before tying his
body to a chair, lowering him down the well.

> *of communism in the country. Never give*
> *the slightest chance for the dark ideology*
> *to rise, even if it is only in our minds.*

Research Process

The name that belonged to my ancestors
never belonged to me. When mother took
me to Perth, Australia, she miswrote
my name. Security stopped and pulled us
at immigration. Separated for
what seemed like an eternity. Mother,
guilty of not knowing the burden her
child was carrying. I no longer called
myself Chandra. There, taped to a cassette:
my lost name. Begging to be listened to.
Take the cassette, hold it between index
and thumb, then slide it inside the player.
Close the archive's door. Adjust the earphones.
Grab a pen and notebook. Press play.

V

Indonesia the Great, be free! Be free!
Long live Indonesia the Great!

—Indonesia Raya, refrain (cont.)

Annotations

I miss texting you after a long night of walking in the rain

I miss saying I'm home regardless of time and day

I miss driving you to work early in the morning, my body on autopilot

I miss texting *I miss you* after spending another night at a house party without talking to anybody

I miss resting my head on your lap, or the other way around, as we prepare to end our day

I miss picking you up from work despite the sea of metal that is Jakarta's traffic

I miss listening to you ramble about your many friends

I miss cooking for you, even though I didn't do it as often as I should've

I miss sharing a plate of roast chicken over noodles

I miss looking forward to desserts, es campur and martabak

I miss spending the Saturday doing nothing together

I miss getting voice notes from you: your confessions, your singing

I miss listening to you sing in the shower

I miss the calmness and authority in your voice, like waves meeting the shore

I miss shopping for the most useless things with you

I miss watching you try hoodies and dresses

I miss you watching me try new formal shirts that I couldn't afford

I miss driving to nowhere in particular at 2 a.m., looking for ice cream, looking for snacks

I miss walking the dog late at night around the neighborhood together

I miss sharing the bed with you and the dog; she leaves barely enough space for one more person

I miss telling you to look at the moon as we stroll in the dark

I miss kissing you on the forehead after an argument to show I still care

I miss gaining weight and not caring, despite everyone's comments

I miss playing guitar as you sing, laughing at every failed chord

I miss slow dancing in the living room past midnight

I miss not being alone when I can't get out of bed

I miss saying my daily goodnights

I miss boiling eggs for breakfast, slicing apples for juice

I miss telling you to rest in bed as I boil water for tea and get the porridge ready

I miss being in your orbit, seeing you dance, hearing you sing

I miss seeing you from the other side of the room as I try to write

I miss writing together, the words eluding us with every glance we take

I miss reading next to you, the dog next to us

I miss not caring because I thought I had everything I needed

I miss having everything

September 30, 2020

So what does the 1965 mass violence mean for contemporary Indonesians, living in a post-authoritarian society, with its dynamic economy, its political challenges between democracy and resurgent populism, and its religious tensions? An early post–New Order opinion survey appeared to show that most people still accepted the New Order narrative of gratitude for the elimination of an atheistic ideology.

—MARTIJN EICKHOFF, ET AL.,
"1965 TODAY: LIVING WITH THE INDONESIAN MASSACRES"

on the 55th anniversary of Gestapu.

Not all of the dead are heroes.
We commemorate seven names,
but a million others fell like
ill chickens, dying unremembered.

While we commemorate seven names,
collective amnesia erases
the ill chickens, deaths unremembered,
excused, preceded by a pretext.

Collective amnesia erases:
the opportunist was waiting,
an excuse to kill, a pretext—
his eyes stayed open during prayer.

The opportunist was waiting:
a snake in the temple garden,
the only opened eye during prayer.
His sins, in the end, forgotten.

Snakes live in the temple garden,
bellies fat with stocks of plunder,
and their sins remain forgotten.
No one there fears God's judgment.

Bellies fat with stocks of plunder,
they tell us to half-staff our flag
to remember God's judgement.
Once a year, our rulers brag,

they tell us to half-staff our flag.
Like donkeys, we follow the tale.
Once a year, our rulers brag,
and we're supposed to remember.

Like donkeys, we follow the tale:
how millions among us fell
and we're not supposed to remember.
Not all of the dead are heroes.

Apologia

I have no thoughts on apologizing. To this day, I haven't thought of apologizing.
—JOKO WIDODO, 7TH PRESIDENT OF INDONESIA,
ON THE 50TH YEAR ANNIVERSARY OF GESTAPU, 2015

We have turned
our backs

on the oceans,

on the echoes

in the seas.

We try not
to remember

the faces

in the waves,

the spirit

of our fellow

countrymen.

We urge
their presence

to sail towards

                              the tides,

                                                towards freedom.

              As for us,
our country

                                        will never

              have   peace.

Stillness, Silence

Kebencian takkan pernah menang karena / beberapa orang memaafkan
— .FEAST, "BERITA KEHILANGAN"

Empty is the body that drinks from the river
of silence—the river whose stream flows
unseen and without sound.

> *During this chaos in 1965 . . .*
> *I could collapse, or I could grow.*
> *If I still keep the hatred,*
> *it's like I have a bomb inside me.*
> *I think I have suffered enough,*
> *why should I suffer more?*

What is forgiveness, if not letting
go of one's self? What is forgiveness,
if not surrendering to silence?

> *Something that cheered us up . . .*
> *was when a squad of guards*
> *came to the barracks. They asked*
> *our forgiveness because they had often*
> *punished us. They asked for our blessing*
> *because they were being sent off to East Timor.*

Souls, your children forgive you
for leaving. They forgive your killers
for their deeds.

> *I live in two sides, two worlds,*
> *the dark world and the light world . . .*
> *When the negative power comes . . .*
> *I really want to . . . take revenge.*
> *But if I can just stay positive and control myself,*
> *I can reach the light again.*

Souls, go in peace
to a place where you can sing.

Blood Letting

Through lush meadows, muddy
rice fields, rice terraces, through
              stone wells, leaf-flooded creeks,
          mangrove trees, through the mangoes
         both ripe and bruised, carried
           by the torrential rain, through
rivers flowing freely
  as a goddess' hair, through
             scores of wetlands and swamps,
         through caverns where djinns took
         firstborns as offerings,
           through firstborns and their fathers,
   through neighborhoods, their dark
corners, through the temple gates,
             church walls, and masjid doors,
        through the fishing villages,
        their floating markets, through
          the reed baskets of tuna,
pomfret, and anchovies,
   through the hidden serpentine
           roads leading to mountains,
        through the mountains, their misty
        peaks and passages, pines
          and ponds, through the craters, blue
   embers, old ashes, through
twisting stone valleys, their streams,
then back through the rivers,

now haunted, now bright red, now
                through palm trees, cold sands, reefs,
        all those waves, away from here,
        let blood flow, let it pass,
                until it glows in the sad
        horizon,
    in scarlet birds,
the crimson sun.

Diorama of Ghosts

1.

Do not say something happened; do not say nothing
happened. You visit the museum at Lubang Buaya

where your government decided: everything
that has to, will happen, in its own time. Everything

that had to, was there, since the beginning of time.
"This is what happened." An undisputed argument.

You circle the outside first, the lawn and garden. You see
the command post, the torturing verandah, the public kitchen,

and the well of death—from which the crocodile's pit
earned its name. This is the house the rebels used to plot

the kidnapping of your generals. This is the verandah
the rebels used to arrest and torture your generals.

This is the kitchen where the women prepared meals
for the rebels. And this is the well where the rebels dumped

your generals' bodies. Each site is filled with dummies.
The rebels: faces full of bloodlust. The generals: helpless,

stripped to briefs and bare chests. Each figure frozen
in time, forever remembered in fervor or fear. At the top

of the stairs, statues of the seven generals remain,
and on top of them stands the giant Garuda,

its wings spread, its chest donning the Pancasila shield,
its tridactyl feet resting on a scroll inscribed with the national

motto: *Bhinneka Tunggal Ika*, Unity in Diversity.

2.

You enter the museum, a static voice recorder on loop
greets you, its age probably twice yours.

The corridors are dim and cold, they showcase
the dioramas of communists, one next to another. Each

with a plaque explaining what they did, where,
when (but never why). Small figurines of men

torturing or killing other men in fields and streets,
while brown tropical trees, clear sky, and white colonial

houses decorate the scene. The said killers look similar
to their larger counterparts outside, furious, bloodthirsty,

ready to kill. After reaching the upper floor and crossing
the skywalk, you enter the next building, where the dioramas

grow large again. You read a sign that says: *The threat
against the ideology of Pancasila is a matter of survival*

*to the nation and state of Indonesia. The museum is built
as one of the means to remind people of Indonesia*

that there is a danger of latent communism. Behind each
glass is a room depicting how your generals were kidnapped

from their homes, still in their nightwear and sandals. This
is what Gestapu means, the kidnappings and subsequent murders

of your generals. This. *Gerakan September Tiga Puluh*,
the 30th September Movement. This. The killings.

3.

The generals, the generals—our revolutionary soldiers.
Not the massacre, not the millions murdered in retaliation,

not the mass starvations, mass sexual assaults, soldiers
shooting the masses, not the religious orators

advocating their congregation to kill their infidel neighbors
by the masses, not the millions more imprisoned without

charge or trial, all cramped in a tight space like chickens
in a coop, not the torturing of the masses, not the orphans

re-educated and forcibly moved into foster families
who killed their biological parents, not the rivers

massed with bodies, not the mountains and forest turned
into mass graves, not the masses of political prisoners

left to starve on Buru island, not the masses today
worshipping whiteness and money, because

the Westerners saved us from Communism, not
the income inequality that continues to sprawl after,

not the racial hatred that still soars to this day.
You can go on, but you're already at the museum's exit.

The exit sign says: *Thank you for witnessing
the dioramas regarding this barbarous incident.*

Do not let something like this happen again.
Enough blood and tears have fallen in our Motherland.

Therefore, guard and maintain our national unity.
Farewell and Merdeka! You exit, the sun greets your skin.

Research Process

The Dutch colonials

have left our country,

but their ideologies persist.

We hate

the air, but still, we keep

breathing.

When people can't kill

your ideas,   they kill

you instead.   Truth?

Truth doesn't exist.   Manipulated   by those in power.

"How did you feel, all those years in prison?"

the interviewer asks.

Prison? In prison, there was no sorrow

among us.

Annotations

Now that you have found
someone else, it's safe to part
here. I wish you all
that I couldn't give. This is
where the last funeral ends.

What stresses me the most is that maybe my words have begun to lose their capability to touch your heart and logic, especially when you're thinking about how my parents view you.

I know you're not me. God, of course, I know that. But every time I try to tell you the facts, you shove me away. It's like you're giving hints that you're giving up on us because we can never get married because of my parents.

That's not true, but you won't listen. You just won't listen because you're tired. You say you want to marry me, but I don't know, you just say what you want without considering how your fiancée feels.

Then, you're back to feeling tired of what you can't have because of your low self-esteem and self-worth (even though you can have it if you just stop, breathe, and listen to your true voice).

And that's it. Case closed. I can't speak because your cramped thoughts matter more than what's true in front of you.

—TEXT FROM THE AUTHOR'S EX-FIANCÉE, AUG. 21, 2019

Afterword

Pieces of history, no matter how distant, together make up the tapestry of our world, within which we all exist. Many Indonesians today argue that the "fear the communists" narrative was necessary to unite the country against a perceived common enemy. Yet, what transpired was not war; it was one-sided killings, a massacre.

Discourse concerning communism in present-day Indonesia upholds the idea of the "danger of this dark ideology" even though the supposed enemies no longer exist. Consequently, a majority of the entire country continues to condemn the victims of the 1965 massacre. These victims include farmers who received the occasional distribution of supplies, artists affiliated with the LEKRA (*Lembaga Kebudajaan Rakjat* or "Institute for the People's Culture") literary movement, progressive women in Gerwani (*Gerakan Wanita Indonesia*, "Indonesian Women's Movement"), ethnic Chinese who were automatically labeled as communists, and thousands of ordinary people like you and me who were caught in the bloodbath.

The older generation of Indonesians often resort to collective amnesia, avoiding any mention of the massacre, lest they dehisce the country's scar from the bloodletting. In an ideal world with reconciliation efforts, there would be no need for these poems. To this day, there exists a black hole of silence in Indonesia's socio-political climate when it comes to acknowledging the tragedy as what it truly was—a tragedy. My poems do not aim to erase or replace the monument of history, but they urge us to consider all its facets, even those that are only visible from a disquieting angle. That is all they ask: to examine the full picture.

Notes

Indonesia Raya

Indonesia's national anthem, written by Wage Rudolf Soepratman on Oct. 28, 1928, and first published by the Chinese-owned newspaper *Sin Po* in the following month, 17 years before Indonesia's independence. *Sin Po* was shut down on Oct. 1, 1965.

Origin of a Disaster

The epigraph was excerpted from Stanley Karnow's news article titled "First Report on Horror in Indonesia", published in *The Washington Post* on Apr. 17, 1966. The article was perhaps one of the first few firsthand pieces of evidence on the massacre presented to the outside world.

"Rumah-rumah adat" translates to traditional houses.

"Sujud" refers to praying in a prostate position.

Death List

The epigraph was excerpted from Kathy Kadane's article titled "U.S. Officials' Lists Aided Indonesian Bloodbath in '60s", published in *The Washington Post* on May 21, 1990.

Killing System

The epigraph was excerpted from Fealy, Greg, and Katharine McGregor. "Chapter 5: East Java and the Role of Nahdlatul Ulama in the 1965–66 Anti-Communist Violence." *The Contours of Mass Violence in Indonesia, 1965–1968*, edited by Douglas Kammen and Katherine McGregor, NUS Press, 2012, p. 124.

Numbers, Statistics, Etc.
Sarwo Edhie Wibowo was an Indonesian Army special forces (RPKAD) commander. The epigraph taken from Permadi SH, quoted in *50 Tahun Indonesia Merdeka Dan Problem Tapol/Napol*, edited by Coki Naipospos, Masyarakat Indonesia untuk Kemanusiaan, 1995, p. 59.

Testimony / Propaganda
The poem's epigraph was excerpted from the above "Airgram A-398", sent from U.S. Department of State to U.S. Embassy Jakarta on Dec. 17, 1965.

Interrogation Room
"Communists don't believe in God"—a phrase commonly found on propaganda signs; the phrase remains used in present-day conversations to justify the massacre.

"Ekor pari" is a whip made out of a stingray tail.

Research Process [One book cites a library]
The library mentioned in the poem is *Institut Sejarah Sosial Indonesia* (ISSI), located in Jakarta. ISSI has an archive of oral interviews with 1965 massacre survivors. Their mission statement is to "promote a greater awareness of history in Indonesia."

1965, Indonesia
The epigraph was excerpted from Roosa, John. "The Movement as a Pretext." *Pretext for Mass Murder*, University of Wisconsin Press, 2006.

Sukarno's quote and full speech can be found in Triyana, Bonnie, and Budi Setiyono. *Revolusi Belum Selesai: Kumpulan Pidato Presiden Soekarno, 30 September 1965, Pelengkap Nawaksara*. Serambi Ilmu Semesta, 2014.

The Sinner's Mantra

The epigraph was excerpted from Mehr, Nathaniel. "Chapter 5: 'The Greatest Prize'—Reflections on the Indonesian Killings." *'Constructive Bloodbath' in Indonesia: The United States, Britain and the Mass Killings of 1965–66*, Spokesman Books, 2009, p. 119.

Genjer-Genjer

"Genjer-Genjer" is an Osing Language folk song from East Java, Indonesia, written by Muhammad Arief in 1942 during the Japanese occupation. The song tells the story about an aquatic vegetable called genjer (*Limnocharis flava* or water spinach) that grows in the wild and how it is used as food by poor people in Indonesia. The song was sung during the Communist Party rallies after it was popularized by Bing Slamet and Lilis Sulyani in 1962.

According to the Indonesian Army's fabricated narrative, Gerwani women tortured the kidnapped generals and danced naked around them while singing "Genjer Genjer".

The song was banned by Suharto's New Order regime, and anyone who played, recorded, or sang the song would be subject to suspicion with affiliations to the Communist Party and often arrested.

Muhammad Arief was captured and imprisoned by the military in October 1965 and presumably died or was killed during his time in prison.

Gerwani and its members remained forever tainted as traitors to the nation because of their ties to the Communist Party.

The first verse translates to:
> Genjer-genjer growing in the fields
> Genjer-genjer growing in the fields
> The mother of the boy gathers genjer
> The mother of the boy gathers genjer
> Taking a bunch she turns away without looking
> Now the leaves are carried home

Mass Murder

The epigraph was excerpted from Kammen, Douglas Anton, and Katharine E. McGregor. "Chapter 1: Introduction: The Contours of Mass Violence in Indonesia, 1965–68." *The Contours of Mass Violence in Indonesia, 1965–1968*, NUS Press, 2012, p. 10.

Holy Duty

The first epigraph was excerpted from Greg Fealy's article titled, "Killing for God," published in *Inside Indonesia* on May 24, 2010.

The second epigraph was excerpted from Ted Yates' film, *Indonesia: The Troubled Victory*, produced by National Broadcasting Company in 1967.

The third epigraph was excerpted from Budiarjo, Carmel. "Chapter 19: The Isolation Block." *Surviving Indonesia's Gulag: A Western Woman Tells Her Story*, Cassell, 1996, p. 164. Carmel Budiardjo was the founder of TAPOL (abbreviation of "Political Prisoners"), an organization that campaigns for human rights, peace, and democracy in Indonesia. Carmel passed away on July 10, 2021.

To Kill a Chicken

The poem's inscription and backdrop are from "Telegram 184A", one of the many declassified U.S documents concerning the 1965 Indonesian massacre, sent from the American Consulate in Medan to the U.S. Embassy in Jakarta on Dec. 6, 1965.

Temple Gate

"Madewa pitra" was mentioned in Mary Ida Bagus' essay, "Transcending Transgressions with Transgression: Inheriting Forsaken Souls in Bali." *Celebrating Transgression: Method and Politics in Anthropological Studies of Culture: A Book in Honour of KLAUS Peter Köpping*, edited by Ursula Rao and John Hutnyk, Berghahn Books, 2006.

Daily Portion

The first epigraph was based on a quote from a former Banser member (*Barisan Ansor Serbaguna* or "Multipurpose Ansor Front"), an Islamic militia organization in Indonesia affiliated with the Nahdlatul Ulama (NU). The former member was quoted in a cable, Telegram 15R, sent from U.S. State Department to U.S. Consular in Surabaya on Jan. 19, 1966.

The second epigraph was from an interview which can be found in Gareth Evans' news article, "Obituary: Anwar Congo, the Mass Killer Who Re-Enacted His Crimes." *BBC News*, Nov. 3, 2019.

Reports on the Land

The poem borrows language found in various reports given by the authorities regarding the massacre:

Telegram 183, from U.S. Embassy in Jakarta to Secretary of State, Dec. 26, 1965.

Airgram A-353, from U.S. Embassy Jakarta to State, Nov. 30, 1965.

Telegram 187, from American Consulate Surabaya to U.S Embassy Jakarta, Dec. 7, 1965.

Yates, Ted. Interview with Rata. *Indonesia: The Troubled Victory*. NBC, 1967.

Oppenheimer, Joshua. Interview with various killers in *The Act of Killing* (2012) and *The Look of Silence* (2014).

The Land's Testimony

The epigraph was taken from Joshua Oppenheimer's documentary, *The Look of Silence*, Final Cut for Real ApS, 2014.

[   ]

The poem's backdrop is taken from the above "Airgram A-353", sent from American Consulate in Medan to the U.S. Embassy in Jakarta, on Nov. 30, 1965.

Red All Over

The epigraph was taken from Joshua Oppenheimer's documentary, *The Act of Killing*, Final Cut for Real ApS, 2012.

Nrimo

The epigraph was taken from Joshua Oppenheimer's 2012 documentary, *The Act of Killing* (Production company: Final Cut for Real ApS). The title of the poem was excerpted from the Javanese philosophy of accepting one's fate or destiny.

Public Knowledge

Richard Cabot Howland was a Foreign Service Officer who was stationed in Jakarta from 1965–1966 at the U.S. Embassy in Indonesia. The first epigraph comes from his article, which was published in the classified internal journal of the Central Intelligence Agency, *Studies in Intelligence* ("The Lessons of the September 30 Affair," vol. 14, Fall 1970, pp.13–28). The article was approved for declassification and release to the public in 1994 by the CIA and is available at the National Archives and Records Administration, RG 263, CIA Records, *Studies in Intelligence*.

The second epigraph comes from Martens, Robert J. "Account of Indonesia Killings Highly Flawed." *The Buffalo News*, 12 June 1990. The piece was a response to Kathy Kadane's "U.S. Officials' Lists Aided Indonesian Bloodbath in '60s" article.

Islands of Souls

Bali, Sumatra, and Java are the three main islands in Indonesia where many parts of the land were used as both execution sites and mass gravesites during the 1965 massacre.

The italicized lines from the first section were inspired by Ted Yates' *Indonesia, the Troubled Victory*.

The italicized lines from the second section were inspired by Joshua Oppenheimer's *The Look of Silence*.

The film mentioned in "Esok: Java" refers to *Pengkhianatan G30S/PKI* (The Betrayal of the Communists), a propaganda film directed by Arifin C. Noer that justifies the 1965 massacre. The earlier mentioned details about Gerwani women torturing the kidnapped generals while dancing naked and singing "Genjer-Genjer" were depicted in the film. The film was mandatory viewing for school students during the New Order era (1966-1998), despite its misrepresentation of history. The italicized lines in the third section were pulled from this film.

"Kemarin," "Kini," and "Esok" mean "Yesterday," "Today," and "Tomorrow" respectively.

"Astaghfirullah" is a short prayer of forgiveness in Islam.

September 30, 2020

Gestapu refers to "Gerakan September Tiga Puluh" or the Thirtieth of September Movement. The movement was used by Suharto (the 2nd president and dictator who stripped Sukarno of his power) as a pretext to set the massacre in motion.

The epigraph was excerpted from Eickhoff, Martijn, et al. "1965 Today: Living with the Indonesian Massacres." *Journal of Genocide Research*, vol. 19, no. 4, 2017, pp. 449–464.

The survey mentioned was from Mohamad, Goenawan, "Remembering the Left," in *Indonesia Today: Challenges of History*, ed. Grayson Lloyd and Shannon Smith (Singapore: Institute of Southeast Asian Studies, 2001), pp. 126–135.

Apologia

The epigraph—Joko Widodo's speech on the 50-year anniversary of Gestapu in 2015—can be found in Humas. "Presiden Tegaskan Tidak Akan Minta Maaf Kepada Keluarga PKI." *www.setkab.go.id*, Oct. 1, 2015.

Consequently, the poem is an erasure based on a translation of Joko Widodo's 2014 inauguration speech, with the line placement reorganized. The full speech can be found in: https://www.rappler.com/world/72529-text-jokowi -inauguration-speech/

Stillness, Silence

The epigraph comes from .Feast. "Berita Kehilangan." *Beberapa Orang Memaafkan*, Sun Eater, 2018 (an Indonesian rock song). The epigraph translates to: "Hatred will never win because / some will always forgive."

The italicized lines from the stanzas come from, in order of appearance:

Lemelson, Robert. Interview with Lanny. *40 Years of Silence: An Indonesian Tragedy*. Elemental Productions, 2009.

Leo, quoted in Sukanta, Putu Oka. "Chapter 9: Niko: Clarity at Last." *Breaking the Silence: Survivors Speak about 1965–66 Violence in Indonesia*, Monash University, 2014, p. 77.

Lemelson, Robert. Interview with Budi.

Diorama of Ghosts

The museum mentioned in the poem is called *Museum Pengkhianatan PKI*, located on the outskirts of Jakarta, near a military air force base.

Lubang Buaya translates as "Crocodile's Pit."

"Garuda" is a mythological eagle-like bird that serves as Vishnu's mount. Garuda is also the emblem of "Pancasila," the foundational philosophy of Indonesia containing five principles.

"Merdeka" is an Indonesian term for the proclamation of independence.

Research Process [The Dutch colonials]

The last poem in the sequence is an erasure/found language from the oral interview with "Chandra" in Jakarta, interviewed by a member of ISSI. The full interview can be found in ISSI's archive, one of the many that are available in the library.

Acknowledgments

I'm indebted to the editors of *Quarterly West*, where some of the poems in this manuscript have appeared as a chapbook, *Blood·Letting*, selected as a runner-up by Luther Hughes for the 2022 Chapbook Contest. Special thanks to Audrey Bauman for editing the chapbook from start to finish.

I'm thankful to the editors of the following journals where these poems were originally published:

december: "Origin of a Disaster," "To Kill a Chicken," and "Island of Souls"
The Iowa Review: "The Land's Testimony"
Snapdragon: "Annotations [Tonight, I can't carry my country's sins]"

My gratitude to Divya Victor for selecting my work as the recipient of the 2023 Gaudy Boy Poetry Book Prize and for exemplifying, through her own work, the poetic wisdom I strive to emulate.

This project wouldn't have been possible without the courage of those who shared their testimony and experience; you are owed so much. A thousand thanks to all the writers and researchers who came before me, whose investment in history laid the foundation for truth and reconciliation, whose work also informed mine. Thank you to Pak Kosim for his patience as I perused ISSI library for hours during the pandemic.

Thank you to my parents for instilling me with the gift of curiosity and for trusting me to walk my own path. Thank you to every Indonesian I've encountered who shared their perspectives, accounts, and understanding of our history. A heartfelt appreciation to my friends for their eternal spiritual support. A special mention to my "Uprising" colleagues—we're in this together.

My deepest gratitude to the Singapore Unbound and Gaudy Boy team for bringing this book to the world. You all have shown so much care and grace. I cannot thank you all enough.

I owe this book to my ex-fiancée, who encouraged me to pursue the truth, without whom I wouldn't have had the courage to peel the layers of our country's history in search of a deeper understanding of our shared past.

About the Author

photo by: Jingrun Lin

Jeddie Sophronius is the author of the poetry collections *Happy Poems & Other Lies* (Codhill Press, 2024), *Love & Sambal* (The Word Works, 2024), and the chapbook *Blood·Letting* (Quarterly West, 2023), a runner-up for Quarterly West's 2022 Chapbook Contest.

A Chinese-Indonesian writer, educator, and translator originally from Jakarta, he received his B.A. in English: Creative Writing from Western Michigan University and his M.F.A. from the University of Virginia, where he served as the editor of *Meridian*. Their poems have appeared in *The Cincinnati Review*, *The Iowa Review*, *Prairie Schooner*, and elsewhere, while their prose is forthcoming in *The Third Coast* and *The Arkansas International*.

They currently live and teach in Charlottesville, VA. They divide their time between Indonesia and the United States. Read more of their work at nakedcentaur.com.

From the Latin *gaudium*, meaning "joy," Gaudy Boy publishes books that delight readers with the various powers of art. The name is taken from the poem "Gaudy Turnout," by Singaporean poet Arthur Yap, about his time abroad in Leeds, the United Kingdom. Similarly inspired by such diasporic wanderings and migrations, Gaudy Boy brings literary works by authors of Asian heritage to the attention of an American audience and beyond. Established in 2018 as the imprint of the New York City–based literary nonprofit Singapore Unbound, we publish poetry, fiction, and literary nonfiction.

Visit our website at www.singaporeunbound.org/gaudyboy.

Winners of the Gaudy Boy Poetry Book Prize

Waking Up to the Pattern Left by a Snail Overnight: Poems
by Jim Pascual Agustin

Time Regime: Poems
by Jhani Randhawa

Object Permanence: Poems
by Nica Bengzon

Play for Time: Poems
by Paula Mendoza

Autobiography of Horse: A Poem
by Jenifer Sang Eun Park

The Experiment of the Tropics: Poems
by Lawrence Lacambra Ypil

Fiction and Nonfiction

Lovelier, Lonelier: A Novel
by Daryl Qilin Yam

Bengal Hound: A Novel
by Rahad Abir

The Infinite Library and Other Stories
by Victor Fernando R. Ocampo

The Sweetest Fruits: A Novel
by Monique Truong

And the Walls Come Crumbling Down
by Tania De Rozario

The Foley Artist: Stories
by Ricco Villanueva Siasoco

Malay Sketches: Stories
by Alfian Sa'at

Other Series

New Singapore Poetries
edited by Marylyn Tan and Jee Leong Koh

Suspect: Volume 1, Year 1
edited by Jee Leong Koh

From Gaudy Boy Translates

Picking off new shoots will not stop the spring:
Witness Poems and Essays from Burma/Myanmar 1988–2021
edited by Ko Ko Thett and Brian Haman

Amanat: Women's Writing from Kazakhstan
edited by Zaure Batayeva and Shelley Fairweather-Vega

Ulirát: Best Contemporary Stories in Translation from the Philippines
edited by Tilde Acuña, John Bengan, Daryll Delgado, Amado Anthony G.
Mendoza III, and Kristine Ong Muslim

Books by our other imprint, Bench Press

Snow at 5 PM: Translations of an Insignificant Japanese Poet
by Jee Leong Koh

Seven Studies for a Self-Portrait: Poems
by Jee Leong Koh

Equal to the Earth: Poems
by Jee Leong Koh

Lightly in the Good of Day: Poems
by Bob Hart

Try to Have Your Writing Make Sense:
The Quintessential PFFA Anthology: Poems
edited by Donna Smith and Howard Miller

Printed in the USA
CPSIA information can be obtained
at www.ICGtesting.com
CBHW020029100924
14328CB00032B/493